LOTTY'S WAR

BY GIULIANO CRISPINI

SERVING THEATRE

SF

SINCE 1830

WWW.SAMUELFRENCH.CO.UK
WWW.SAMUELFRENCH.COM

AUTHOR'S NOTE

On 28th July 1940, German forces bombed the harbour of St Peter Port on the island of Guernsey. Abandoned by the British government islanders caught by the advancing enemy endured five years of occupation. They had to learn to live, work and survive with their captors.

This play is about what it is to be human in the throes of war. It explores where the moral lines between what is right and what is wrong blur.

It asks the question, "What would you have done?"

Giuliano Crispini

ABOUT THE AUTHOR

GIULIANO CRISPINI

Giuliano is a writer, director and producer. He trained at the Liverpool Institute for Performing Arts and has gone on to work on many projects throughout the UK in TV, film and theatre.

A special mention must be given to Clare Slater, who helped *Lotty* on her journey with her incredible dramaturgic skills.

For Guernsey and all its forgotten heroes

The first draft of the play was produced on the island of Guernsey at the Princess Centre for Performing Arts in 2008.

Charlotte (Lotty) Hervé – **Katie Howell**
Ben De Carteret – **James Joyce**
General Rolf Bernberg – **Michael Fenner**

Directed by **Iain Davie**
Set by **David Crisp**
Lighting by **Julian Adams**

Cast of the 2016 touring production:

Charlotte (Lotty) Hervé – **Victoria Emslie**
Ben De Carteret – **Mat Ruttle**
General Rolf Bernberg – **Ian Reddington**

Understudy Lotty and Ghost – **Daisy Ward**
Understudy Ben De Carteret – **James G Nunn**
Understudy General Rolf Bernberg – **Nick Warnford**

Original Director – **Bruce Guthrie**
Associate Director – **Carla Kingham**
Dramaturg – **Clare Slater**
Set Design – **Victoria Spearing**
Costume Design – **Suzie Tidy**
Sound Design – **Mike Walker**
Lighting Design – **Elanor Higgins**
Guernsey Patois Translations – **Hazel Tomlinson**

CHARACTERS

CHARLOTTE HERVÉ Lotty. Guernsey girl. Seventeen years old at the start of the war.

ROLF BERNBURG A general of the occupational forces. Forty one years old at the start of the war.

BEN DE CARTERET Guernsey boy. Seventeen years old at the start of the war.

GHOST A seventeen-year-old Slavic worker.

SETTING

A house on the island of Guernsey, 1940–1945.

The Bailiwick of Jersey and Bailiwick of Guernsey are two British Crown dependencies in the English Channel, near the coast of Normandy. The Channel Islands were the only part of the British Isles to be invaded and occupied by German forces during World War II.

SCRIPT NOTE

A . indicates a beat, an unsaid thought.

Scene Two

1st July 1940. Four days later.

LOTTY and BEN are dressed in black. Plates and bottles and food leftovers are everywhere. LOTTY is tidying up as the radio plays.

BEN Veis-tu tous ches restànts. *[Look at all these leftovers.]*

LOTTY I'll take some to Mrs Wilson later tonight.

BEN You can't be out at night now.

LOTTY Of course I can.

BEN You can't, it's not safe.

LOTTY Well that's just ridiculous. What is some German soldier going to do if he sees me carrying a plate of ham sandwiches at dusk?

BEN .

Give Mrs Wilson a drink and there is no stopping her. When she laughs she sounds like that puppy of hers barking.

.

LOTTY I can't get his face out of my head. It didn't look like him. None of them looked like, people, any more.

BEN The Germans will be called to account, just like last time.

But for now they're here. They've said they will leave us alone if we –

LOTTY Oh come on! How can you believe that? They were given these islands and the cowards couldn't help themselves. Couldn't help having a bit of target practice…

BEN Please calm down –

LOTTY Don't tell me what to do –

.

They are both beaten.

.

BEN Why didn't you get on the boat with your mum, last week?

Did you stay because of me?

The song on the radio finishes. For a moment it's quiet.

LOTTY I stayed because I didn't want to leave my dad. And because of you.

A new song begins. She kisses him kindly.

And because there was a bumper crop this year, so the island couldn't afford to lose its fastest picker. War or no war.

BEN I'm glad you stayed.

LOTTY You wouldn't cope without me.

Do you think there's any hope of us leaving?

BEN The harbour was destroyed in the raid. It's just you and me now.

LOTTY And your mum.

BEN What German wouldn't be scared of her? Things could be worse. Besides, we have each other, you know, we're family…

LOTTY Pass me those plates please?

He picks up plates from the table and passes them to her.

BEN …so I was thinking, why not make it official?

LOTTY I'm a bit old to be adopted.

She turns to **BEN**.

BEN *gets down on one knee.*

Oh my God –

BEN I'll make you so happy.

LOTTY Ben. This is too much.

BEN No, you're right. Sorry I just thought, perhaps something positive.

LOTTY It's my dad's funeral…

BEN Of course… Sorry. Sleep on it.

LOTTY Thank you.

She kisses him on the cheek.

BEN Let's just get your things and get to mine before dusk.

.

LOTTY I'm staying here.

BEN My mum's expecting us.

I said that we –

LOTTY I live here, Ben.

BEN Well, after everything… I thought…

LOTTY It's a very kind offer, but I'd prefer to stay here.

BEN Lotty – I don't think that's a great idea – not now they're on the island –

LOTTY This is my house, Ben. I was born upstairs. This is my house.

.

BEN How about I run and get some bits, and I stay here tonight too? Just until… For now.

To keep you company. I'll sleep down here in the armchair...

LOTTY We'll both sleep upstairs. I'll sleep in Dad's bedroom. You can take mine.

.

BEN Right.

I am not going to let anything happen to you.

I'll be back as soon as I can.

LOTTY I'd be back faster.

BEN I know you would.

> **BEN** *exits through the kitchen door.* **LOTTY** *is very much alone. The radio music is sad, but comforting.*
>
> *She continues to clear and gets taken up with the music. She dances a little. She turns around, and sees a tall, handsome* **GERMAN GENERAL** *in the other doorway.* **LOTTY** *screams. She instinctively grabs the knife by her side and stands squarely in defence of her kitchen.*
>
> *The* **GENERAL** *doesn't blink.*
>
> *They stare at each other, neither moving.*
>
> *The* **GENERAL** *breaks the stand-off by gently reaching out and turning off the radio.* **LOTTY** *flinches.*

GENERAL Good evening.

> *He speaks with a German accent, but his English is good. He sounds friendly.*

You live in an occupied territory and you leave your front door open? I know it's an Open Island now, but nonetheless...

LOTTY Get out of my house.

GENERAL My name is General Bernberg.

LOTTY Get out!

GENERAL What's yours?

> **LOTTY** *steps forward, with the knife at arm's length.*

I don't think you should be playing with that.

LOTTY Get out of my house.

GENERAL Get out of my house, General Bernberg, sir.

If you refuse to introduce yourself, then this will certainly be harder.

Your house has been commandeered as my personal residence. I believe your Government sent you a note?

LOTTY A note?

GENERAL Of instructions. Did you not receive it?

LOTTY No. I've been busy.

GENERAL I would prefer it if you put the knife down.

Somehow he wins.

Now – you realise you are trespassing. Are you going to leave or shall I have you removed?

LOTTY I live here.

.

GENERAL Who else lives here?

LOTTY Just me.

.

GENERAL I do need a housekeeper and I shall need breakfast and dinner cooked daily.

LOTTY No.

GENERAL No?

LOTTY No.

GENERAL You refuse?

LOTTY Yes.

GENERAL Don't you like your home? What's wrong with it?

LOTTY I love my home very much.

GENERAL I'm doing you a service. You get to stay in the place you love and make sure it's kept in order.

LOTTY This is my home, it is not for sale, it is not for rent and it certainly is not here to be, commandeered.

GENERAL I see. You won't mind if I get a second opinion?

The **GENERAL** *drags a previously hidden and petrified* **BEN** *into the kitchen from the hallway.*

LOTTY Ben –

BEN Lotty…

LOTTY If you dare touch him I'll –

GENERAL Before we say anything we regret I shall make a proposal. I shall stay here as your guest. In return, I shall arrange for the protection of your home. And your friend.

LOTTY I will not serve a Nazi.

The **GENERAL** *turns, dragging* **BEN**.

BEN No –

LOTTY Have the house. I'll collect my things.

GENERAL That is not the proposal. Do as you are told and we shall live peacefully. Cause me trouble and there will be consequences. Do you understand?

.

.

An uneasy understanding passes between the **GENERAL** *and* **LOTTY**.

Good.

The **GENERAL** *throws* **BEN** *in the direction of the front door. We hear him run out and slam it behind him.*

.

The **GENERAL** *looks around. Opens the pantry cupboard. Inspects the back door's lock.*

My bag is outside.

.

.

Begrudgingly, **LOTTY** *exits towards the front door. The* **GENERAL** *takes his first seat in his new home.*

.

LOTTY *enters with the bag.*

Danke schön.

.

I will need something to eat. What do you have?

LOTTY There's some sandwiches…and gâche.

GENERAL Gâche?

She points at the fruit bread.

The remains of a feast.

.

The **GENERAL** *takes a bottle of wine out of his bag. No one moves.* **LOTTY** *realises that she's meant to prepare this meal. Reluctantly, she gets a plate and a glass. She gathers some sandwiches and pours a glass of wine. She* *is shaking. She goes to put the bottle back on the table and knocks the full glass over.*

LOTTY Sorry! …General Bernberg… Sir.

.

GENERAL These things happen.

.

No one moves. **LOTTY** *is expected to clear up the mess. Eventually, reluctantly, she does so.*

You haven't told me your name.

LOTTY Charlotte Hervé.

GENERAL Charlotte.

LOTTY *brings over the sandwiches.*

Excellent. I shall call you Charlotte and you will call me General.

LOTTY *(exploding:)* You have no right –

GENERAL I have every right, Charlotte. This is our island now.

You should go to bed now.

.

LOTTY *doesn't know what to say. She starts to leave the kitchen.*

I'll take the master bedroom.

A distorted refrain from the earlier radio music, disintegrating into white noise.

Scene Three

9th July 1940. The next morning.

LOTTY *is drinking tea at the kitchen table. Alone. Has she slept at all?*

The **GENERAL** *enters from the hallway.*

He sits at the head of the table.

GENERAL Good morning.

LOTTY *stares at him.*

Coffee please.

LOTTY *stares at him.*

.

Thank you.

.

She stands to fetch the coffee.

White noise.

Scene Four

10th July 1940. The next morning.

LOTTY *is drinking tea at the kitchen table. Alone. Has she slept at all?*

The **GENERAL** *enters from the hallway.*

He sits at the head of the table.

GENERAL Good morning.

LOTTY *stares at him.*

.

She stands to fetch the coffee.

Thank you.

White noise.

Scene Five

11th July 1940. The next morning.

LOTTY *is staring out of the kitchen window. Alone. Has she slept at all?*

The **GENERAL** *enters from the hallway.*

GENERAL Good –

LOTTY *(without turning around:)* Coffee's on the table.

GENERAL Thank you.

He sits at the head of the table. Takes a sip. It doesn't taste good.

LOTTY *looks at the radio. Turns it on. A happy tune.*

Disintegrates into white noise, halting music and broken news reports slowly fuse back together as the radio tells us that war continues on the continent, and on the occupied island of Guernsey.

Scene Six

12th September 1940. Two months later.

LOTTY *is frying bacon and eggs. Badly. She is paying much more attention to the BBC news report on the radio. It cuts out at a crucial moment. She picks it up, opens up the back, fiddles with a wire, it jumps back in.*

The **GENERAL** *enters, buttoning up his cuffs, and inspects his cremated breakfast in the frying pan.*

GENERAL Good morning.

Did you sleep well?

He turns off the radio. **LOTTY** *stiffens, before serving him coffee.*

I did also.

Danke.

LOTTY *serves the breakfast. It looks awful. He tastes. She watches.*

Salt, please.

LOTTY *passes the salt.*

Sit.

LOTTY *doesn't sit.*

Are you not hungry?

There's plenty of food.

This silence every morning is quite unappetizing.

LOTTY I've nothing to say.

GENERAL I find that hard to believe.

.

.

LOTTY Fine – where is it you go every day?

GENERAL I'm sorry?

LOTTY Where do you go? When your officers pick you up each morning? Do you walk the piers? Sit in the tearoom and watch the world go by? Stand on the corner of Fountain Street and terrify people? What do you do?

GENERAL What do you do every day?

.

LOTTY Very little.

GENERAL Listen to music?

.

I have an office. A control point.

LOTTY Where is it?

Is it a secret?

GENERAL No. I believe it was the Bailiff's office.

LOTTY And where's he now? The traitor…

GENERAL He was a sensible man –

LOTTY He turned the island over –

GENERAL He was a sensible man. Who no longer has an office.

.

LOTTY What's it like, in town?

GENERAL Normal.

LOTTY How do you know what normal is like here?

GENERAL It is the same everywhere. People go to work. People go home. It's normal.

LOTTY It isn't normal for Guernsey to be occupied. Watched and guarded –

GENERAL Did you not have laws before? Police?

The rules are just different now.

LOTTY The Guerns won't just have rolled over. We're fighters –

GENERAL No. Guernsey is Germany now. It was handed over, without a fight. Most people have decided to recognise the changed situation, and are adapting.

LOTTY Most?

GENERAL A small handful still need persuading.

LOTTY Good for them.

.

GENERAL Some of your fellow islanders tried to escape to England in a fishing boat yesterday. All access to vessels will be denied from now on.

LOTTY What will happen to them?

GENERAL The perpetrators will be executed.

Maybe people will think twice.

LOTTY Do you know their names?

GENERAL What does it matter?

LOTTY They'll have families, and friends. They're people . . .

GENERAL I do not. I have bigger things with which to concern myself. These eggs are overcooked.

LOTTY I'll cook them less tomorrow.

GENERAL And my boots need polishing.

LOTTY Yes, general.

GENERAL   See how much better it is to have a bit of conversation over breakfast?

LOTTY Yes, general.

GENERAL It's a fine day today. It would be good for you to go into town.

LOTTY Really? Today? That would be – thank you.

.

These past weeks, I've longed to paddle in Fermain Bay –

GENERAL You can't go there.

LOTTY But – you allow me out but you forbid me –

GENERAL All the beaches have been mined.

LOTTY Oh.

GENERAL So don't go there.

LOTTY No.

GENERAL I have never locked the door, Charlotte.

LOTTY No, because you always carry a gun. Like your hobnailed patrol outside.

GENERAL "Hob-nailed"?

LOTTY Their boots. Clip-clopping around my house every hour.

GENERAL Ah yes, schuhnagel. Hob-nailed. I see. Today one of my officers will drive you into town, where you will get a ration book.

LOTTY What?

GENERAL Everyone on the island is now being rationed.

LOTTY Even the Germans?

GENERAL No, we have our own supply lines.

LOTTY Of course. Different rules.

General, I would prefer to walk into town.

GENERAL One of my officers will drive you.

LOTTY But I would prefer to –

GENERAL You will be driven.

LOTTY The whole island will see me…

GENERAL In a German military car?

LOTTY In a stolen car with a swastika on it –

GENERAL They will be jealous. Civilians on the island

are no longer allowed to drive.

LOTTY Since when?

GENERAL Since people started attempting to escape. And since we learned that there are British military personnel hiding on the island.

LOTTY There are?

GENERAL We believe they are being helped by islanders. So we must restrict everyone's freedom until they have been found.

You will also register for your ID card today.

LOTTY Yes, general.

LOTTY May I do a little shopping?

GENERAL What do you need?

LOTTY Some stockings and…

GENERAL And…

LOTTY Other things…

I need to go to Boots…the chemist…for ladies provisions.

GENERAL Of course. You could pick me up some of those Guernsey sweets all the men are talking about. And if you learn of anything when you're in town, about these spies, I will naturally want to hear about it.

LOTTY I will not help you.

Car engine noise off. The **GENERAL** *gets up to leave. He smiles.*

GENERAL I will want dinner by seven. Remember to put the clock forward by two hours tonight. As of midnight we will be running on German time.

The **GENERAL** *exits, leaving behind a half-eaten breakfast.*

It is quiet once again. **LOTTY** *throws the food away. She turns on the radio, catches the positive tones of some British propaganda. She switches it off.*

She spots the **GENERAL***'s military coat hanging on the back of his chair. Her first reaction is to chase after him. A reaction she is swiftly ashamed of. It dawns on* **LOTTY** *what she is looking at.*

She picks it up.

She puts it back down again.

She looks over in the direction of the front door. She looks out of the kitchen window.

She sits back at the kitchen table.

LOTTY *slips her hand into one of the coat pockets. Some money. A used handkerchief. She tries the inside pocket. Pulls out a folded set of papers – all in German. She tries to read them nonetheless.*

Something catches her eye. A repeated word. A familiar name.

BEN Lotty?

LOTTY jumps a mile. The papers go flying. BEN has snuck into the kitchen door.

LOTTY Oh my God. Ben. Oh my God.

BEN *(hushed and hurried:)* Are you alright?

LOTTY No I am not alright. I thought you were the general.

BEN No. It's just me. Hello.

LOTTY Hello.

.

BEN How are you?

LOTTY I don't know.

BEN Has he hurt you?

LOTTY No.

.

.

What happened to you? It's been sixty-six days. Since you were here last.

.

BEN I know.

I've been running the yard for you. The crop's

been picked.

LOTTY Thanks.

BEN The crop's been picked. It took almost five weeks.

LOTTY That's because I wasn't there.

BEN Probably. We had to. They were rotting on the vines and the price we were able to get for them! Your dad would have been over the moon.

LOTTY What's happening? In town? On the rest of the island?

BEN Everything. Nothing. It's almost normal. Except the Germans drive on the right. The island feels, inside out.

LOTTY Can't you all fight?

BEN The bailiff's saying we should "passively cooperate" since London's doing nothing for us. The Jerries are on their doorstep, and they're doing nothing. They've cut us adrift –

LOTTY Who needs London?

.

Why didn't you come sooner?

BEN There's always a guard here. I've been watching, to try and see you through the kitchen window. I've learned their patrol patterns, and you can hear their boots a mile off. Listen, we've got to move quickly. Is there anything you need?

LOTTY What do you mean?

BEN I'm getting you out of here.

LOTTY I can't leave Ben. He'll be furious.

BEN I'll hide you.

LOTTY He knows your name, remember? You haven't thought this through. He's told me about executing the fishermen, who attempted to escape.

BEN What? They weren't caught.

LOTTY I don't understand.

BEN   They set off from *La Vieille* and slipped right underneath the nose of a patrol boat. It was brilliant. By the time the Germans realised, they were nearly in Dover.

LOTTY But. Why would he lie?

BEN We're at war – everyone's lying.

LOTTY Even so, no risks, no plans, not even for me. I can look after myself.

BEN Lotty –

LOTTY And look.

> **LOTTY** *shows* **BEN** *the paperwork.*

This is all military stuff.

BEN It's also all in German.

LOTTY I know.

BEN So what can we do with it? Come on, let's go…

LOTTY Look closer. The word *Spitzel.* There. And there. And there. I think it means spy.

BEN Could mean something else.

LOTTY And next to it –

BEN Symons. Something something Symons.

LOTTY That's got to be Mark. You know, from school? Went off to the army? Now Corporal Mark Symons?

BEN Maybe.

LOTTY General Bernberg said that there are British soldiers hiding on the island. I think Symons is one of them.

BEN So why haven't they found him?

LOTTY He's hiding. And I bet I know where. He and I used to make dens in the cricket scoreboard. You know, behind the numbers.

Ben?

BEN I remember Mark Symons. Obviously. He never left you alone.

LOTTY Oh, Ben, come on.

BEN Just because his family was English and I was born over there, he thought we were best friends. He was an idiot.

LOTTY Ben –

BEN And the way he was so, smug, about signing up straight away. Not up for it, de Carteret? Not for King and country?

This island's my country.

LOTTY Ben, please. Would you go, to the cricket pitch, and find out if he's there? I bet he is. You could take him some food. See how to help him.

.

BEN Ok. Well, I guess we could go.

LOTTY We? No, just you. I'm staying here. Who knows what else the general will leave lying around.

BEN Lotty – you're insane.

> **LOTTY** *replaces the papers.* **BEN** *crouches under the kitchen window, peeping out.*

Look we've got to go in the next thirty seconds. The shift change will be nearly done.

LOTTY I'm not leaving. This is my father's house. I am not letting them take it over.

BEN Lotty, please.

LOTTY You can come back, we'll need to set up a signal so you know when it's safe to come in.

LOTTY *looks around. She has an idea.*

We'll use my dad's radio.

BEN Really?

LOTTY It's a transceiver.

BEN What?

LOTTY He modified it to communicate with the lifeboat station. His radio can do both, transmit and receive. I can send out a pulse signal.

BEN But the lifeboat station's been shut down. No one's allowed –

LOTTY The frequency will still exist. Just find a receiver –

BEN Lotty...

LOTTY I'll try it tonight. When it's safe to come back. Listen out. The pulse will be...two bleeps – for "Lot-ty". Over and over.

BEN I don't know...

LOTTY Ben. Get food. Go to the cricket ground. And then find a radio.

BEN Fine. Ok.

He kisses her.

·

She kisses him back.

LOTTY Go.

BEN *cautiously opens the kitchen door, listens, and dashes out.* LOTTY *softly shuts the door.*

.

A car door slams outside in the driveway. **LOTTY** *jumps again. She scrambles to put the papers back inside the coat pocket.*

Just as the **GENERAL** *re-enters. He picks up his coat.*

Forget something?

She takes his coat over and puts it on his shoulders.

GENERAL Thank you. Take your coat when you go into town later. It's cold outside.

LOTTY Yes, general.

The **GENERAL** *exits.* **LOTTY** *smiles to herself. There's a thrill in the air.*

Transition A

*A sense of time passing, of the radio being used as a
signaling device many times, with "Lot-ty" echoing over
the radio waves, and a handful of midnight meetings
between* **LOTTY** *and* **BEN**. *He brings news. She shares
secrets.*

They are a team. It is serious.

It is also quite fun.

Crackly Christmas music.

Scene Seven

23rd December 1940. Evening. Three and a half months later.

The **GENERAL** *is sitting at the kitchen table, with his papers. Further down the table,* **LOTTY** *is cutting something up. "Silent Night" comes on the radio. The* **GENERAL** *starts to hum along, despite himself.* **LOTTY** *looks across at him. He becomes self-conscious.*

GENERAL It's German.

They continue their work.

Eventually, **LOTTY** *unfolds her masterpiece: a chain of Christmas trees cut out from stuck together tomato paper. She places a chair against the kitchen dresser and starts to climb up, to hang the decorations. The chair wobbles.*

LOTTY Oh.

The **GENERAL** *notices, and gets up to steady her chair. They're very close together.*

Thank you.

GENERAL They're very nice.

He helps her finish the job in awkward silence.

LOTTY I love Christmas trees.

GENERAL They're German too – originally. Perhaps I could get one tomorrow.

.

I'd like more coffee.

LOTTY There's none left.

GENERAL Then I will try your tea.

LOTTY It's really only dust now.

GENERAL A small cup will do.

> **LOTTY** *makes a pot of tea. She is careful with her rations.*

LOTTY Someone in the shop today told me that you have announced an amnesty for any spies on the island.

GENERAL That is correct.

LOTTY Do you really think there are some? After all this time?

GENERAL I'm sorry?

LOTTY You must be certain there were spies in the first place, to hold an amnesty.

GENERAL I am. And they continue to make my life, complicated. Someone must be sheltering them. I have declared a Christmas amnesty to allow them to turn themselves in.

.

LOTTY What are you going to do with them?

GENERAL They will be protected by the Geneva Convention. Their rights will be respected and they shall be treated as prisoners of war.

LOTTY Oh.

So you wouldn't shoot them?

GENERAL Not if they turn themselves over in the next – eleven hours, and ten minutes.

LOTTY I see. That's good.

GENERAL We can't have trained enemy agents running all over the island. People will get hurt unnecessarily, and no one wants that.

LOTTY No. Ok.

She smiles.

GENERAL What is it?

LOTTY It's just. It's nice when something fair happens. Basic common sense seems to have been lost recently.

.

GENERAL We cannot change which side we are on. But whilst we are in this house, we are just two people.

I would like it if you didn't hate me.

.

LOTTY I don't.

.

The lights flicker off and on.

The new curfew. Power will be shut off in two minutes.

Gathering his papers.

Goodnight, Charlotte.

The **GENERAL** *exits.* **LOTTY** *turns off the music, and sits in silence, looking at her Christmas decorations.*

She prepares the paraffin lamp near the back door. With some doubt, she goes to the radio-transmitter, and sends out the signal. "**LOTTY**".

The lights snap out, but her signalling continues.

The radio signal fuses into a ticking clock.

Scene Eight

17th December 1940. Pre-dawn. A few hours later.

Darkness still, except for a shaft of moonlight through the kitchen window. **LOTTY** *is asleep, her head on the table.*

The back door slips open, **BEN** *is in the doorway. His movements are swift and assured – he's done this plenty of times. He closes the curtain, lights the paraffin lamp dimly.*

He wakes **LOTTY** *gently. He goes to kiss her, but she's too sleepy and doesn't see the gesture.*

Without words, they secure the kitchen for another midnight meeting. Hushed, and once they feel safe:.

BEN You've decorated.

LOTTY You took longer than usual.

BEN I was stopped by a soldier just before the curfew, and then couldn't get to him until nearly midnight. Symon's leg is getting much worse. He can't move it at all now.

LOTTY I stole the last of the general's morphine two days ago. Is there anyone else who might have some?

BEN I'm not sure. I don't like to ask around too much.

pause

LOTTY *begins to go about their routine, getting bean jar out of the pantry, wrapping up some bread.*

LOTTY It gets less every week.

BEN For everyone. Thank you.

My mum says hello.

LOTTY Tell her I miss her too.

Listen, Ben. You know this amnesty.

.

BEN Yes.

LOTTY Have you told Symons?

BEN No.

LOTTY I think you should.

BEN We can't hand him in, Lotty.

LOTTY No, no, it's not that.

I think he should hand himself in.

BEN What? Why? It was your idea to help him in the first place. I've been risking my neck for months to –

LOTTY And that's been brilliant. But aren't you worried?

BEN Of course. Of course I'm worried.

LOTTY But what if we're doing him more harm than good? What if he gets caught? Or you get caught?

BEN I won't –

LOTTY But what if –

BEN Lotty –

LOTTY The general says no spies will get hurt if they hands themselves in today.

BEN Why were you talking about the amnesty with him?

LOTTY It came up –

BEN You've got to be more careful, Lotty.

LOTTY He'll be treated as a prisoner of war if he hands himself in during this amnesty. He won't be killed. It's a code of honour.

BEN Honour?

LOTTY Ben – I believe him.

.

Hey – don't you dare – for one minute – think that
I am, that I am – sympathising – with them, or whatever.
But we have to face facts. This war isn't going our way,
we could be stuck with them on a permanent basis.

.

BEN So he just hands himself in? Walks up to the Germans
like some kind of Christmas present?

LOTTY And stays safe. Yes.

Just give him the option. Please.

LOTTY *kisses* **BEN**.

The electricity snaps back on. The room lights up.

We see the **GENERAL** *standing in the hallway door,
hidden from sight.*

Oh my God.

LOTTY *and* **BEN** *jump to turn the lights off quickly.
They don't see the* **GENERAL**.

.

*Back in the dark, apart from the paraffin lamp glow,
they both listen silently for some time. They hear nothing.*

BEN It must be nearly dawn. I should go.

BEN *listens at the back door, and slips it open.*

LOTTY Speak to him, Ben.

And, if he does go, tell him to arrive in uniform. There
will be no mistakes that way.

BEN *leaves.* **LOTTY** *looks out the window after him. She
turns the paraffin lamp up stronger. The* **GENERAL** *is
no longer in the doorway.* **LOTTY** *heads upstairs to bed.*

Perhaps sound of the sea fading into a Christmas carol, into radio voices, and a BBC news story fades in about captured German POWs being treated well in Britain.

Scene Nine

18th December 1940. Early evening.

An undressed, neglected Christmas tree leans in the corner. The **GENERAL** *and* **LOTTY** *are mid stand-off.*

LOTTY You promised that wouldn't happen!

GENERAL I did no such thing.

LOTTY You stood there and promised: no harm would come to anyone who handed themselves in.

GENERAL He has not been harmed.

LOTTY You're deporting him to Germany!

GENERAL To a prisoner of war camp, yes. As I told you.

LOTTY You said nothing about a camp.

GENERAL What did you think? I would keep a British serviceman here on an island full of British people. I have not broken any promises.

Do you know him?

LOTTY No.

GENERAL Why are you so upset?

LOTTY I thought I could trust you.

GENERAL Someone was harbouring the spy. If the people of Guernsey continue to plot against Germany, if they whisper in the dark against us, there will be repercussions.

He takes the radio from the stand.

LOTTY What are you doing?

GENERAL I thought you understood this war. I thought you listened to your radio, to the BBC…

He rips open the back of the radio.

LOTTY It's just music…

GENERAL You cannot be trusted. The people of Guernsey cannot be trusted.

He tears out the inside of the radio, destroying it.

.

.

All radios are being confiscated. I think it best this one isn't found don't you?

Silence.

I am not sure why you are so protective of this island.

LOTTY It's my home.

GENERAL Take a look out of your kitchen door.

LOTTY *is exhausted and confused. She slowly crosses the kitchen and opens the back door. We see that it is now painted with a graffiti "V"*

LOTTY I don't understand.

GENERAL They are everywhere in town today. "V" for victory, we believe. Scrawled across all German property – my car had the same treatment. I won't bother with an amnesty next time.

LOTTY It's Churchill's symbol. Anti-Nazi. Why is it on my house?

GENERAL I think you know why.

LOTTY I haven't done anything wrong.

GENERAL I'll have my men clean it off.

LOTTY No! Let it stay if that's what the islanders want. If that's what they believe.

I have only ever tried to – fine! Damn them all.

GENERAL closes the door, takes the key from its hook, locks the door, and pockets it.

GENERAL I think this will be better for everyone.

LOTTY Are you keeping me in, or them out?

LOTTY has no strength left to fight. She starts to cry, and this upsets her even more. She forces herself to stop.

GENERAL Don't you like the tree? It took one of my officers all day to find one.

LOTTY Christmas is for children. I am not a child.

GENERAL I never thought you were.

.

Here, have some wine with me.

The GENERAL gets a bottle and pours them both a glass. LOTTY is unsure.

Let's just pretend.

.

LOTTY takes the glass.

Prost.

LOTTY Prost.

They drink.

.

.

I don't know your name. You have lived in my house for half a year, and I don't know your first name.

.

GENERAL Rolf. Rolf Bernberg. Nice to meet you.

> **ROLF** *extends his hand for a handshake.* **LOTTY**
> *hesitates. She shakes his hand.*

LOTTY I don't owe you anything.

ROLF No.

.

LOTTY How do you sleep at night, Rolf?

.

ROLF I don't think anyone sleeps well any more.

LOTTY But you must know what you are doing is wrong. Destroying people's lives, killing them, behaving like beasts.

ROLF You see this only from your point of view. Imagine if England had lost the Great War. Imagine they were blamed for it. Their country destroyed, their colonies and land taken away from them. You and your children and your children's children, made to pay for all the damage done, for generations. Wouldn't you think that at least a little unfair?

LOTTY But you started it and we had to beat you, just like we're going to beat you now.

ROLF It is the winners who write history. Please do not always believe everything you are told.

All I know is that in Germany life was hell. We had six million unemployed. People starving on the streets, because France and England were taking everything we worked for. You must agree it is our right to work hard, to feed ourselves, to have enough space to grow as a nation.

Just like your British Empire. The greatest empire ever known; where the sun does not set.

Who are the beasts now?

LOTTY That's completely different…we were civilised.

ROLF Have I not been civilised to you?

They drink **ROLF***'s wine together in silence.*

.

.

LOTTY You killed my father.

When you bombed Saint Peter Port, in July, a week before you arrived. He had just seen a boat of children off to England.

The island had already been given over to you.

But you bombed us anyway.

ROLF Geneva hadn't told us yet.

LOTTY I could barely recognise him. Afterwards.

I won't ever forget that smell.

.

ROLF I didn't know.

LOTTY You ordered the bombing.

ROLF No. It doesn't work like that.

LOTTY How does it work?

ROLF We believed the trucks at the port to be a military target.

LOTTY Forty-five minutes you attacked for. Couldn't you tell after five that we weren't firing back?

We buried my dad, the day you came here.

.

.

Do you miss your family?

ROLF My parents died a long time ago. My brother in the Great War.

LOTTY Your wife? Girlfriend?

ROLF Stop it now.

LOTTY I'm only asking…

ROLF I said stop.

.

It's us who survive that are the victims, not the dead. They're just ghosts.

The lights flicker once again, signalling the imminent power cut.

.

Tomorrow – will you go to the pantomime with me?

LOTTY They're going ahead with it?

ROLF Yes, the Regal players have insisted, for Christmas. I'm not sure what I'm going to make of it, I've never been to one before.

LOTTY Oh it's wonderful! We go every year.

ROLF Then it's settled. A Christmas outing.

LOTTY Islanders can't sit with the Germans.

ROLF I'm a general. Yes you can.

LOTTY I don't think it's a good idea –

ROLF – it was just an idea. Never mind.

I'm sorry.

Charlotte –

I'm sorry. About your father.

.

ROLF *drains his wine glass. Getting up to go to bed.*

LOTTY It's Lotty. No one calls me Charlotte.

.

ROLF *takes the key to the kitchen door out of his pocket, and puts it on the table.*

A silence. The radio is broken.

BEN I'm not asking you to do anything you haven't already done.

They hear movement upstairs. **ROLF** *is out of bed.*

LOTTY Go –

BEN *looks out of the window.*

BEN I can't – the patrol.

LOTTY Quick –

LOTTY *opens the pantry cupboard door. It's considerably emptier than six months ago.* **BEN** *climbs in and* **LOTTY** *shuts the door. She runs to the kitchen door, but fails to lock it in time.*

ROLF *(offstage)* Lotty?

LOTTY Yes?

LOTTY *turns up the paraffin lamp for more light as* **ROLF** *enters from the hallway, in his pyjamas.*

ROLF You're up.

LOTTY So are you.

ROLF *(noticing the door is unlocked and open)* Is everything ok?

LOTTY Thought I heard something outside. Must have been the patrol.

.

Both become aware that **LOTTY** *is in her nightdress only. They are both barefoot and vulnerable.*

What are you doing up?

ROLF It's Christmas morning. I thought I would surprise you by making you breakfast.

Pancakes!

LOTTY You cook?

ROLF Better than you.

He begins searching for pans and ingredients. He is dangerously close to finding **BEN**.

LOTTY Let me do that…

ROLF Nonsense. It is my turn to treat you.

Wait…

ROLF walks towards the pantry. **LOTTY** *holds her breath. But he reaches into the cupboard next door and pulls out a brown paper package.*

Ta da!

LOTTY Oh –

ROLF Well open it then!

LOTTY Yes. Yes, of course.

ROLF enjoys watching **LOTTY** *open it. A bright red dress.*

Goodness. Rolf – thank you.

Where on earth did you get it?

ROLF I hope it fits. I think it will.

LOTTY It's wonderful. I love it! I'm going to try it on.

ROLF Well go on then.

LOTTY dashes out into the hallway. **ROLF** *is left grinning.*

ROLF and **BEN** *occupy the same space, for quite some time.*

LOTTY returns, looking gorgeous in this simple but flattering dress. Still barefoot. They stare at each other.

Can you –?

The dress zip needs fastening. **ROLF** *does it up, a bit fingers and thumbs.*

How do I look?

ROLF Lieblich.

LOTTY I do have a little something for you.

It's nothing compared to this. A bit feeble actually.

LOTTY *hands him a little paper bag she has got from one of the pots on the window sill.*

ROLF Guernsey sweets!

This is the most wonderful gift I have ever received.

.

LOTTY *quickly kisses* **ROLF** *on the cheek.*

LOTTY Danke schön.

ROLF Bitte schön.

LOTTY Rolf, I –

ROLF *kisses her, wholeheartedly.*

He has surprised himself. He's embarrassed.

LOTTY *kisses him in return. It becomes more than a kiss. She pulls away.*

I –

ROLF Sorry –

LOTTY No. Please don't be.

We shouldn't.

.

ROLF The boy.

LOTTY That was different. He's like, a brother, really.

ROLF You love him.

LOTTY He was born in England. Will he get deported?

ROLF Yes.

LOTTY Why?

ROLF Let's not –

LOTTY Rolf, please…

.

ROLF England is holding a lot of German nationals. The Führer has ordered that all British nationals be taken to Germany. To be used as bargaining chips.

LOTTY Is he in danger, then?

Touching **ROLF***'s arm.*

Please, this time –

ROLF Yes.

LOTTY Well then stop it. Don't send them.

ROLF I can't just ignore orders.

LOTTY The first day you came here, you promised to protect him. That was our deal.

.

ROLF You're asking me to defy orders.

LOTTY I'm asking you to do the right thing.

.

.

ROLF Five hundred will be on a boat next week. But your friend… I'll make sure he's not on it.

LOTTY Thank you, Rolf.

They kiss again. Six months of loneliness and emotion are shared and something very real passes between them.

ROLF *leads* **LOTTY** *to the bedroom. She stops at the top of the stairs.* **BEN** *emerges from the cupboard. They look at each other, before she carries on.*

ROLF *unzips* **LOTTY**'s *new dress.* **BEN** *and* **LOTTY** *stare at each other briefly, before he slips out of the unlocked door.*

Continued silence. The radio is still broken.

Interval.

ACT TWO

Scene One

1st January 1945. Morning. Four years later.

Still no music and no radio. The house is freezing.

ROLF is attempting to make toast against a candle. He is older, more tired. LOTTY enters from the hallway. She is older, more beautiful.

LOTTY Oh, the smell of toast…

ROLF Ich wusste es würde dich wecken. *[I knew it would wake you.]*

LOTTY Du kennst mich zu gut. *[You know me too well.]* You're wasting the candle.

ROLF A treat every now and then… I loathe stale bread.

LOTTY I know you do.

LOTTY kisses ROLF.

I'm sorry I overslept.

ROLF We were up late. It was a beautiful sunrise.

LOTTY Wasn't it? A promise for the year ahead.

ROLF You say that every year. Here.

Sharing his toast, they sit at the kitchen table.

I have something for you. A new year's treat. Close your eyes.

LOTTY Rolf –

ROLF Ich sagte, schließ die Augen! *[I said, keep your eyes shut!]*

> **ROLF** *takes a knife. Scrapes it up and down the toast.*

LOTTY What are you doing?

ROLF Ssh.

> *The scraping continues.*

Now then. Open your mouth.

> *He puts the slice of toast in front of her mouth.*

Bite.

> **LOTTY** *bites. Eats.*

What do you taste?

LOTTY Stale, cold toast.

ROLF Try again.

What you do you want to taste?

.

LOTTY Butter. Hot butter. Hot-butter-soaked-toast.

And jam.

ROLF What flavour?

LOTTY Strawberry. Sticky sweet. With bitter little pips.

> *She opens her eyes.*

I adore you. Dank dir, Liebster. *[Thank you, darling.]*

> **LOTTY** *kisses* **ROLF**.

ROLF Was würden Sie für Schokolade tun? *[What would you do for chocolate?]*

ROLF *turns to a pile of paperwork.*

LOTTY We said, Rolf. Not at breakfast.

It's New Year's Day.

ROLF I still have to work.

LOTTY Rolf –

Playfully, LOTTY *takes a sheet away from him and reads it.*

I don't know this word – selbstmord.

ROLF You shouldn't read my paperwork.

LOTTY Then don't read it at breakfast. What does it mean, "another" what?

.

ROLF Suicide. There were two others last week. And one last month. Usually the young ones.

LOTTY Your men? Why didn't you say?

ROLF What's there to say?

They are finding it, increasingly difficult.

The lack of food is all they talk about. Most haven't had a proper meal since our supply lines were cut.

The locals have more than my soldiers now – it's not right.

LOTTY It'll be spring soon. Maybe we can get the tomato yard going again.

I won't be able to do it by myself. I tried.

ROLF Yes, I know. Sorry.

LOTTY Come on. Chin up. Where's that British stiff upper lip?

.

Scene Four

3rd January 1945. Morning. One day later.

LOTTY *is drinking water at the kitchen table. Alone. Has she slept at all?*

ROLF *enters, doing up his shirt.*

ROLF Good morning, liebster.

LOTTY *stares at him.*

Kissing her on the forehead.

He sits at the head of the table.

Lotty?

LOTTY Good morning.

ROLF Coffee please.

LOTTY *stares at him.*

.

Why did you sleep in your old room?

They look at each other.

.

Silence.

The radio is still broken.

Scene Five

4th January 1945. Morning. One day later.

LOTTY *is drinking water at the kitchen table. Alone. Has she slept at all?*

ROLF *enters, doing up his shirt.*

ROLF Good morning.

LOTTY *stares at him.*

He doesn't kiss her.

He stands at the head of the table.

Charlotte?

.

.

He unhooks his military coat and leaves through the front door.

LOTTY *stares after him.*

We hear the car engine.

.

.

LOTTY *goes to the fireplace, reaches her arm up the chimney and pulls out a bundle wrapped in sooty cloth. She unwraps it on the table. It's just about recognisable as her father's old radio. Frankenstein-like, it's being haphazardly re-built.* **LOTTY** *sits at the head of the table and determinedly sets to work.*

A couple of wire tweaks.

Turns it on.

Nothing.

Silence. The radio is still broken.

Scene Six

4th January 1945. Midnight. A few hours later.

Candlelight. **ROLF**'s *military coat is hanging up.*

LOTTY *is working at the kitchen table, hunched in a shawl over the radio in the cold.*

A couple of wire tweaks.

Turns it on.

It whirs and clicks into action. Music blares on and fills the kitchen for the first time in four years. **LOTTY** *is elated, before quickly turning it down to a whisper.*

Exhausted, comforted, she listens.

She re-tunes it. Snippets of the BBC – she has been starved of news for so long that this is a miracle. She hears about a significant allied victory in Burma. She hears anti-German propaganda.

.

After much consideration, she sends out the "Lot-ty" signal.

It repeats and repeats. It's dizzying.

Scene Seven

11th January 1945. Midnight. One week later.

LOTTY *and* **BEN** *are facing each other for the first time in four years.* **BEN** *has grown into a man – stronger, more assertive, almost dangerous. He has a gun by his side.*

As hushed as ever –.

LOTTY What is that?

BEN Protection.

LOTTY You're a fool, running around the island playing solider.

BEN *starts to leave.*

Ben –

BEN You're the one who signalled to me, Lotty.

LOTTY Yes –

BEN I've not heard from you for four years.

.

LOTTY For a long time I didn't know if you'd been deported after all. But then I spotted your mum in the shop once –

BEN They let us stay at the last minute.

Thanks for that.

.

.

LOTTY Thanks for coming.

BEN One of the lads heard your signal. So.

You look well.

LOTTY Like a whore you mean.

BEN I didn't come here to fight.

LOTTY Like a Jerry-Bag.

BEN Lotty –

LOTTY How's your mum?

BEN Not great. Pretty broken.

LOTTY Any news?

BEN John Le Prevost was shot the other day. For stealing a German radio.

LOTTY Oh.

BEN But I expect you already knew that.

LOTTY You can still trust me Ben. I've never been the enemy.

BEN John was part of GUNS, he was doing good work.

LOTTY GUNS?

BEN It's our underground network. Our resistance. Guernsey Underground News Service.

I run it.

LOTTY You do?

BEN Yes, Lotty, I do. Everyone's a bit older and uglier now.

LOTTY What do you do?

BEN We try and help the ghosts. You know, the slave workers? Soviets and Poles, mainly. You must have seen them, shuffling in lines behind German soldiers, carrying their own body weight in munitions, or stones for the endless fortifications, or whatever the Jerries think they're too good to carry.

.

LOTTY I've seen them.

BEN The prisoners your general brings to the island, and then works to death.

LOTTY He doesn't –

BEN Do you know how many of them have died here?

Do you know what we call Alderney now? Devil's Island.

At the rate of boat trips to Alderney, we estimate over four thousand have died. A year. So far.

LOTTY Do you have proof?

BEN My own eyes prove it to me. Why won't you open yours?

LOTTY Let go.

BEN *realises he is holding her by the wrists. He lets go.*

BEN Sometimes they escape their camps. Risk everything out of desperation to eat. I've hidden a handful of them around the island. Different basements, different sheds. There are three in the cricket scoreboard.

We can none of us understand a word they're saying. But they seem grateful.

.

You have leftovers?

LOTTY Would you like some? We've had no meat for weeks.

BEN *inspects the pot.*

BEN Ham?

.

Peter Duquemin had a nice walk yesterday.

LOTTY Peter Duquemin?

BEN He walked all the way from Fort George to town.

LOTTY And why did he walk all the way from Fort George to town, Ben?

BEN Because he was told to.

LOTTY Who told him to?

BEN Then he got on a boat and sailed away.

LOTTY Ben. Stop.

BEN Peter was arrested and deported yesterday. His family were starving so he killed their pig without permission. He's been deported and the animal confiscated. I imagine that's the beast you enjoyed this evening.

Couldn't quite finish it? Stick in your throat?

LOTTY I didn't know, Ben –

BEN You didn't ask.

LOTTY If food is offered to you, you don't turn it down. You eat. You don't starve. You would have done the same.

BEN I know where my food comes from.

LOTTY Where did they take him?

BEN We're not sure.

LOTTY Maybe I can find out some news about him. I could ask Rolf –

BEN No-one wants his help.

LOTTY He's not a monster, Ben.

He saved you.

.

.

BEN I was… What did you want?

.

LOTTY I've been working on something. A crystal radio set.

BEN We had to learn. After the Jerries confiscated all the radios a few years ago. It was difficult, but we've built loads now, to pick up the BBC. Crystal's are pretty weak, but better than –

As **BEN** *has been talking,* **LOTTY** *has reached up into the chimney breast and pulled out the wrapped-up bundle.*

She carefully places it on the table.

What's that?

LOTTY I built my own proper radio. Out of the bits from my dad's old radio. I couldn't bring myself to throw it away when it broke. When it was broken.

I used to watch Dad fix it, improve it, fix it again. He'd let me help sometimes, connect the copper, make it work.

BEN Can I see it?

LOTTY *unwraps the radio.*

BEN *is quietly impressed.*

Impressive.

LOTTY It was the idea of music again. And a connection, to the world.

BEN Can I turn it on?

LOTTY Quietly.

BEN *turns on the radio, it's very quiet, but it provides a clear, 1945, happy tune. They are both transported, for a moment.*

BEN I've not heard a signal that clear in years.

He turns the dial and the radio crackles, through the BBC, more music, and then a soft, distant voice. BEN *dares to turn it up a notch. A voice speaking German. They are both shocked.*

What's that?

LOTTY *listens carefully.*

LOTTY It must be their communication frequency.

BEN I've never heard that before.

.

LOTTY They're talking about, replacing the beach, something at the beach – more landmines at the beach. Tomorrow.

.

BEN You speak German?

LOTTY You carry a gun.

Have you ever used it? It's been four years, have you killed anyone, Ben?

.

.

BEN What else? What else can you hear?

LOTTY It's all pretty technical, I can't –

BEN What time tomorrow will they be at the beach?

.

LOTTY 9.30pm. Low tide.

BEN This is gold dust. Imagine what else we'll hear.

LOTTY Ben, I'm not –

BEN What?

.

LOTTY I only wanted some music. And to see if you were alright.

BEN Well you've got your music. And I'm just dandy. So let's now concentrate on what matters. My God, Lotty. We've been hostages in our own land. People are stolen in the dead of night, bundled into cars and never heard from again. And we just consider that normal now. You might have been skipping around in silk stockings –

LOTTY Ben, you just don't get it.

BEN I do! This house, this mini patch of Germany is a bruise on our island.

LOTTY But you still came.

Please don't ask me to fight against him.

BEN Your father would be ashamed.

LOTTY *slaps* **BEN**.

.

.

Look. We all just want the right end to this war. I know you want that too.

.

LOTTY Of course.

BEN Well then.

BEN *knows exactly in which drawer to find tomato paper and a pen. He is poised to write.*

Go on.

LOTTY *listens carefully again.*

*The German transmission on the radio grows in volume
and overtakes* **LOTTY***'s translations.*

Transition B

A sense of time passing, of the radio being used as a signaling device many times, with "Lot-ty" echoing over the radio waves, and a handful of midnight meetings between **LOTTY** *and* **BEN**.

They are a team. It is serious.

Eventually some fun between them creeps back in.

The 1945 happy tune fades back in, replaced by a news report of Italy now becoming an ally.

Scene Eight

12th February 1945. Midnight. Six weeks later.

LOTTY, *in low light, is once again hunched against her homemade radio in the cold, scribbling.* **BEN** *is standing over her, blowing warm air on his hands.*

A mumble of German voices on the radio.

BEN Is there much more?

LOTTY Shh!

BEN You need to hurry up.

LOTTY You need to shut up.

.

They're bringing a new shipment of ghosts over on Wednesday, to Fermain Bay. I couldn't tell what time.

BEN We need to know what time –

LOTTY Well I'm sorry but I couldn't catch it. It's not easy.

BEN Tu n'avais pas d'poine d'vànt. *[Guernésiais: You had no trouble before.]*

LOTTY That's different.

Damn it, I've lost it.

BEN Fine. I can get the guys ready by Wednesday. They'll take the ghosts to Le Guet at Cobo. The Jerries always march them through the streets, to humiliate them. To humiliate us, I think, too.

LOTTY What will you do?

BEN Create a distraction. Start a riot, give us a window for the next raid. The more of the Jerries' food we take, and sneak to the ghosts, the more we win. We'll get this printed tonight and start distributing tomorrow.

LOTTY Just don't hurt anyone. Only get the food and go.

BEN We know what we're doing. No-one's been hurt since you've been on board.

LOTTY I just want to help the ghosts.

Do the other islanders know you speak to me? Do they know I'm helping?

Have you told them?

Ben?

BEN Yes. No-one else can speak German as well as you.

LOTTY So...?

They don't trust me, do they?

.

BEN It's not that simple.

LOTTY I think it is.

BEN Lotty. They don't know you like I do. Not any more. We've all had to change. Guerns haven't been kind to Jerry-bags –

To people, mixed up, with the Germans.

LOTTY Mixed up?

BEN I didn't mean that.

LOTTY I never stopped loving you. Despite everything.

BEN I wish I could believe you.

LOTTY Are you telling me you've not found your way into a woman's bed yet?

BEN Lotty –

LOTTY I'm not an idiot, Ben. Look at you.

.

BEN Once they go, it'll be like it always was.

German crackles back on the radio.

LOTTY 2pm on Wednesday. That's the time.

A BBC broadcast blends over the German voices. A report on the allies crossing the Rhine into Germany.

Scene Nine

14th February 1945. Valentine's Day. Afternoon. Two days later.

LOTTY *is listening to music on her radio, wrapped up in her shawl.*

Car engine off.

LOTTY *hurriedly wraps the radio up. There's no time for the chimney breast, so she pushes it to the back of the pantry.*

ROLF *enters.*

LOTTY You're home early.

ROLF I missed you.

He kisses **LOTTY**.

Happy Valentine's Day. It's today, isn't it?

LOTTY You're a fool – you'd never heard of it until you'd met me.

ROLF I think it's a wonderful celebration. A day for the most important person in my life.

LOTTY *smiles at him. She takes off his military coat. She takes off his boots. He's no longer a soldier.*

She kisses him.

LOTTY How come you finished early?

ROLF There was a problem. Another raid of our food stores. It was very well timed. Someone had information.

And then this afternoon one of my soldiers was caught
unleashing a boat in the harbour, trying to escape.

LOTTY What happened?

ROLF I shot him.

LOTTY What? Why?

ROLF He was clearly the informant.

LOTTY You don't know that. It sounds like he was just
frightened.

ROLF It cannot be tolerated. I cannot be seen to tolerate
it.

This all comes down on me you know. It's me who has
to bear the consequences.

What?

.

LOTTY How can you do it?

I could never do it so I need you to tell me. What do
you feel?

Do you feel powerful?

Do you feel guilt?

.

.

What is happening on Alderney? I've heard people
calling it Devil's Island.

ROLF Who have you been talking to?

LOTTY I hear things.

ROLF Alderney is not my responsibility.

LOTTY What about here then? What about the house near
the quarry? Why is there a pile of black boxes piled up
outside?

Wo geht ih hin? Darf ich mitkommen? *[Where are you both going? Can I come?]*

She was bolder than I ever was. She taught me to be bolder. We married ten months later.

We didn't think we could have children.

.

LOTTY I hate you.

I think I hate you.

ROLF I suppose you should.

It's easier to pretend to be someone else when you're at war.

.

.

.

LOTTY Who are you?

You have a son. And a wife. All this time. In our house.

Can't you at least face me? Turn around and face me? Rolf.

ROLF I'm waiting for something.

LOTTY For what?

ROLF For news. For a signal.

.

We heard something today. Some intelligence. We finally got a step ahead, but there's nothing to be done.

You're going to bomb Dresden tonight.

A rumbling of planes overhead, growing louder. Ground-to-air gunfire too.

I had grown tired of Berlin, and its politics, so we all moved.

Erika and Felix live in Dresden. And I'm not home.

ROLF *continues to look up at the sky as Allied planes drone above the house, screaming on their way to a devastating bombing campaign.*

LOTTY Come inside. Shut the door.

LOTTY *pulls* **ROLF** *back into the kitchen, and locks the door. The noise continues, only slightly muffled.*

They sit separately, lost, at the kitchen table. They are both heartbroken.

ROLF *puts his head in his hands. Defeated.*

LOTTY *is torn. She wants to help him.*

She fetches her radio from the pantry. Unwraps it. She turns it on – German voices.

ROLF *looks up. He understands the secret. But he is also surrounded by the voices of his countrymen.*

Both **LOTTY** *and* **ROLF** *listen as German plans are exchanged, panic rising in their voices.*

.

LOTTY *re-tunes to find comfort instead. Sombre, beautiful German orchestral music.* **ROLF** *hears home.* **LOTTY** *crosses the room and puts an arm around him.*

BEN '*s face appears at the kitchen window. He sees* **LOTTY** *and* **ROLF** *but they don't see him.* **BEN** *sees betrayal.*

The planes continue relentlessly overhead.

The music continues. Soaring.

Scene Eleven

15th February 1945. Mid-afternoon. A few hours later.

The radio remains on proud display on the kitchen table.
LOTTY *is listening to a familiar tune, one of her dad's
favourites.*

A note sits at her elbow.

Car engine, off.

ROLF *bursts in from the front door. He throws a bloodied
bag onto the kitchen table.* **LOTTY** *jumps away from it.*

LOTTY What's that?

ROLF Food.

> **ROLF** *shakes off his coat. His hands, arms and shirt are
> covered in blood.*

LOTTY Where did you get it?

ROLF Does it matter?

> **LOTTY** *looks into the bag.*

LOTTY Rolf?

ROLF Just cook it and eat. Or are you too holy to save
yourself from starvation now?

LOTTY We haven't any wood.

ROLF Go to the bake house.

LOTTY It's not open till tomorrow.

ROLF Well burn something! Do you want to eat or not?

LOTTY Tell me where you got it.

ROLF It's that old dog, from down the road.

LOTTY Mrs Wilson's dog?

ROLF We are starving.

LOTTY Rolf –

ROLF The Vega hasn't been for two months. I'm just trying to make sure we survive. Are you really going to refuse to eat it?

.

> **LOTTY** *hands* **ROLF** *the note.*

LOTTY This is for you. Special delivery courtesy of the RAF.

> **ROLF** *reads.*

ROLF In German, how thoughtful.

LOTTY It's a form for unconditional surrender.

It's over Rolf.

ROLF I know.

LOTTY Rolf – last night…

ROLF Last night was only a nightmare.

> **ROLF** *notices his bloodied shirt for the first time. He looks confused.*

LOTTY Have you heard? From…?

Rolf?

> **BEN** *has snuck into the house behind* **LOTTY**. *He is brandishing a gun.*

Ben!

What are you doing?

BEN *(to* **ROLF***:)* Sit down.

> **ROLF** *doesn't move.*

Sit! Now!

BEN *removes the* **GENERAL***'s gun and puts it on the sideboard.*

LOTTY Ben, please.

BEN Haven't you heard Lotty? It's all coming to an end. The allies have bombed Germany, wiped out Dresden! They'll be here soon. To liberate us from these animals.

LOTTY I heard.

BEN But then I thought, how will he pay? For what he did to me. To you. To us? I can't let him off that lightly.

LOTTY Ben you're not a killer.

ROLF The guards are just outside. You fire that gun and your life is over.

BEN Your guards abandoned their post hours ago. There's nothing left to protect you.

LOTTY Ben think about what you're doing. Killing him isn't going to change anything.

BEN You have always thought I was weak, Lotty. Useless. I should have come to save you that very first night.

To **ROLF***, creeping closer.*

Tchique tu y as fait? T'as l'affraont dé m'la halaïr. *[What have you done to her? How dare you take her from me?]*

ROLF I don't understand…

BEN Go on Lotty, translate. Lotty et mé.

.

Go on.

LOTTY Lotty and I.

BEN Nous châre aën passaï. Enn' histouaire. *[We share a past. A history.]*

LOTTY We share a past. A history.

BEN Nous châre enn'île. *[We share an island.]*

LOTTY We share an island.

BEN T'es rian du tout ichin. *[You are nothing here.]*

LOTTY You are nothing here.

BEN T'es battu. *[You are defeated.]*

LOTTY You are defeated.

.

ROLF *(**ROLF** laughs)* But I still had your girl.

> **BEN** *lurches forward. He and* **ROLF** *pounce into a fight.* **BEN** *is younger and stronger.* **ROLF** *is experienced in battle.* **ROLF** *gets the upper hand and seizes* **BEN***'s gun. He goes to shoot him.*

> **LOTTY** *grabs* **ROLF***'s gun. She has never held one before.*

LOTTY Stop it, please!

> *A gun goes off.*

> *All three stand shocked.*

> **ROLF** *falls to the ground.* **LOTTY** *runs to him.*

Rolf… I'm so sorry.

ROLF Lotty, I…

> **ROLF** *dies.*

.

> *She cries.*

.

BEN Lotty…

LOTTY What would my father say?

BEN You did the right thing. You've survived.

The sound of boots running up the path to the front door. Furious knocking.

Lotty.

Come with me. We'll run away together, hide in the cricket score board until the allies come. You'll be a hero.

LOTTY I can't.

BEN It'll be just like it always was. We'll build a new life together. Make a home of our own.

LOTTY This is my home.

.

BEN *exits towards the front door. A door opens. A door closes.*

LOTTY *is alone in the kitchen.*

As before, crackling, low, sombre but beautiful German orchestral music fades up.

End

Property List

Table
Two dining chairs
Sink
Cooker
Bench
Pantry
Table for radio

Act 1

Scene One
1930s radio
Glass of water
Pliers

Scene Two
Plates
Bottles
Food leftovers
Knife
General's bag
Fruit bread
Bottle of wine
Wine glass
Sandwiches

Scene Three
Tea
Coffee

Scene Four
Tea
Coffee

Scene Five
Coffee

Scene Six
Bacon
Frying pan
Eggs
Newspaper
Coffee
Salt
Money
Handkerchief
Papers in German

Scene Seven
Handmade Christmas tree paperchain made from tomato
paper
Pot of tea
Paraffin lamp

Scene Eight
Paraffin lamp
Bear jar
Wrapping
Bread

Scene Nine
Neglected Christmas tree
Door key
Bottle of wine
Two wine glasses

Scene Ten
Paraffin lamp
Tree decorations
Star
Jar of preserved tomatoes
Pans
Various ingredients
Brown paper package containing red dress
Paper bag
Jar of Guernsey sweets

Act Two

Scene One
Toast
Candle
Knife
Pile of German paperwork

Scene Two
Stockings with hole
Needle and thread
Parcel
Stub of candle
Cans of corned mutton, lamb and green peas. Ten ounces of sugar, tea, condensed milk, eight ounces of chocolate
Gun

Scene Three
Glass of water

Scene Four
Glass of water

Scene Five
Glass of water
Radio wrapped in sooty cloth

Scene Six
Candle

Scene Seven
Gun
Pot of leftovers
Tomato paper
Pen

Scene Eight
Tomato paper
Pen

Scene Ten
Cigarette
Lighter

Scene Eleven
Bloodied bag
Note
Gun

Sound Effects

Act One

Scene One
1940s music
Distorted radio crackle
BBC news reports
Bombing/battle/chaos
1940s music

Scene Two
Various 1940s music
Sad but comforting music
White noise

Scene Three
White noise

Scene Four
White noise

Scene Five
Happy 1940s music
White noise with broken news reports and music

Scene Six
BBC news reports
Car engine turns off
British propaganda
Car engine
Car door slam

Transition A
Lotty signal
Crackly Christmas music

Scene Seven
Carol "Silent Night"
Lotty signal
Ticking clock

Scene Eight
Sea fading into a Christmas carol/radio voices/BBC news
reports about prisoners of war

Scene Nine /Scene Ten /
Wind

Act Two

Scene One
Wind

Scene Two
SFX
Scene Three
SFX

Scene Four
SFX

Scene Five
Car engine

Scene Six
Whirring and clicking of radio
1945 music
BBC reports/anti-German propaganda
Lotty signal

Scene Seven
1945 music
BBC/crackle/German voice

Transition B
Lotty signal echoing over the radio
Happy 1945 music
News reports

Scene Eight
German voices on radio
BBC broadcast

Scene Nine
1945 music
Car engine off
White noise

Scene Ten
Planes overhead
Ground to air gunfire
German voices on radio
German orchestral music

Scene Eleven
Familiar tune
Car engine off

Crackling, low, sombre German orchestral music

Lighting

Act One

Scene Seven
The lights flicker off and on
The lights snap out

Scene Eight
Shaft of moonlight
Lights the paraffin lamp dimly
The room lights up
Turn the lights off quickly

Scene Nine
The lights flicker once again, signalling the imminent power cut

Scene Ten
Turns up the paraffin lamp for more light

Act Two

Scene Two
Lights the stub of a candle

Scene Six
Candlelight

Scene Eight
Low light

Scene Ten
Moonlight spills into the room

Lightning Source UK Ltd.
Milton Keynes UK
UKOW06f2355250416

272970UK00001B/7/P